THE POWER OF HELPING HANDS

THE IMPACT OF MUTUAL SUPPORT

DR. JAGADEESH PILLAI

Made with ♥ on the Notion Press Platform
www.notionpress.com

|| Dedicated to all wisdom seekers around the World ||

ଷ

Contents

Contents

PRAYER

"Om Bhadram Karnebhih Shrunuyaama DevaahBhadram Pashyemaakshabhiryajatraah SthirairangaistushtuvaamsastanoobhihVyashema Devahitam YadaayuhSwasti Na Indro VridhashravaahSwasti Nah Pooshaa VishwavedaahSwasti Nastaarkshyo ArishtanemihSwasti No Brihaspatir DadhaatuOm Shantih, Shantih, Shantih"

The literal meaning of this mantra is: OM. O Gods! Let us hear auspicious words from our ears. O reverent Gods! Let us behold propitious visions from our eyes, let our organs and body be stable, healthy, and strong. Let us do that which is pleasing to the gods in the life span allotted to us. May Indra, inscribed in the scriptures, bring us fortune! May Pushan, the knower of the world, grant us prosperity! May Trakshya, who vanquishes enemies, bestow us with blessings! May Brihaspati bring us success!
OM Peace, Peace, Peace.

About The Author

Dr. Jagadeesh Pillai is a renowned Guinness World Record holder, writer, and researcher hailing from Varanasi, also known as the abode of Lord Shiva. With a Ph.D. in Vedic Science and a range of creative ideas and achievements, he is a true polymath. He is the author of more than 100 books including Research Publications. Although his roots can be traced back to Kerala, the people of Varanasi hold him in high regard and affectionately consider him one of their own.

In 1998, Dr. Pillai was offered a job at Banaras Hindu University, but he left the position after only two months to pursue greater goals in life. He believed that in order to study Indian scriptures and engage in other creative endeavours, he needed to retire from the daily grind of working solely for money at a young age.

He started an export business from scratch, using the knowledge he had gained from a previous job in the industry. His intelligence and unique approach to business led to great success in a short period of time, earning him more in just a decade and a half than he would have in a lifetime working in a government job. Upon the passing of Dr. APJ Abdul Kalam, Dr. Pillai decided to leave the business and dedicate himself to reading, studying, researching, and experimenting.

During his tenure in the export business, Dr. Pillai traveled to over 16 countries, gaining valuable insight and experiencing the world and life in detail.

Dr. Pillai has achieved four Guinness World Records in the following subjects:

"Script to Screen" - In this record, Dr. Pillai produced and directed an animation film within the shortest time possible, breaking the previous record set by Canadians. He has also received numerous national and international awards and recognitions for this achievement.

Longest Line of Postcards - For this record, Dr. Pillai created a line of 16,300 postcards on the occasion of the 163rd anniversary of Indian Postal Day. The event also included a questionnaire about the Indian flag.

Largest Poster Awareness Campaign - Dr. Pillai designed an awareness campaign on the subject of "Beti Bachao - Beti Padhao" (Save the Girl Child - Educate the Girl Child) to achieve this record.

Largest Envelope - In tribute to the Indian Prime Minister's "Make in India" initiative, Dr. Pillai created a 4000 square meter envelope using waste paper to achieve this record.

Attempted - **70000 Candles on a 210 kg Cake** - To celebrate the 70th Indian Independence Day, Dr. Pillai attempted to light 70,000 candles on a 210 kg cake, which was recorded in World Records India.

Attempted - **Documentary on Dhamek Stupa of Sarnath in 17 Languages** - Dr. Pillai attempted to create a documentary on the Dhamek Stupa of Sarnath, dubbing it in 17 different languages. The result of this attempt is currently awaiting confirmation from the Guinness World Records.

Dr. Pillai is skilled in teaching the Bhagavad Gita, a Hindu scripture, and is popular among young people. He has helped many young people improve their lives through his motivational teachings.

In addition to teaching, he has composed and sung numerous Sanskrit Bhajans and patriotic songs.

He has also written and directed several short films and documentaries for awareness campaigns, and has volunteered with the police in both UP and Kerala to spread awareness about various issues through videos and photography.

Incredibly, he has produced and directed over 100 documentaries about the city of Varanasi, all on his own.

He has also helped and guided more than 25 boys and girls to achieve world records through creative and innovative methods. He is a multifaceted person who uses his intellect and the blessings given to him by God to excel in various areas. He is both a teacher and a student, always learning and teaching, and is able to master any subject he comes across.

He is a selfless social activist and motivational speaker who has overcome struggles and failures to become a successful and enthusiastic individual with a rich life experience.

In addition to his work with the Bhagavad Gita, he is also an efficient Tarot card reader, Astro-Vastu consultant, and a talented singer and composer. He has sung the entire Ram Charita Manas and Bhagavad Gita in his own compositions, and has sung the phrase "Lokah Samastha Sukhino Bhavantu" in 50 different languages. He is currently working on a detailed and scientific study of Vedas, Upanishads, Puranas, and the Bhagavad Gita. He has also composed and sung the Hanuman Chalisa and Gayatri Mantra in 108 and 1008 different compositions, respectively.

Awards - Four Times Guinness World Records, Winner of Mahatma Gandhi Vishwa Shanti Puraskar, Mahatma Gandhi Global Peace Ambassador, Kashi Ratna Award, Dr. APJ Abdul Kalam Motivational Person of the Year 2017, Mother Teresa Award, Indira Gandhi Priyadarshini Award, Bharat Vikas Ratna Award, Udyog Ratna Award, Vigyan Prasar Award, Poorvanchal Ratn Samman.

Preface

The Power of Helping Hands: The Impact of Mutual Support is a book that explores the profound and far-reaching effects of mutual aid. Through a combination of research, personal stories, and expert insights, this book provides a comprehensive look at the power of helping hands and the positive impact they can have on our lives.

This book is an exploration of the ways in which mutual support can help us to overcome challenges, build resilience, and create meaningful connections with others. It examines the various forms of mutual aid, from informal networks of friends and family to formal organizations and institutions, and how they can be used to create positive change. It also looks at the psychological and social benefits of mutual aid, and how it can be used to foster a sense of belonging and community.

The Power of Helping Hands: The Impact of Mutual Support is a book that will inspire readers to recognize the power of mutual aid and to take action to create a more supportive and connected world. Through its thoughtful and engaging narrative, this book will provide readers with the tools and insights they need to make a difference in their own lives and in the lives of those around them.

I

Introduction to Mutual Support

Mutual support is a powerful tool that can help individuals and groups alike to achieve their goals. It is a form of collaboration that involves individuals or groups working together to achieve a common goal. Mutual support can be used to build relationships, foster collaboration, and create a sense of community.

Mutual support is based on the idea that everyone has something to offer and that everyone can benefit from the support of others. It is a way of working together that encourages individuals to share their knowledge, skills, and resources with each other. Mutual support can be used to create a sense of belonging, foster collaboration, and build relationships.

When engaging in mutual support, it is important to remember that everyone has something to offer and that everyone can benefit from the support of others. It is important to be respectful of each other's contributions and to recognize that everyone has something to gain from the collaboration. Mutual support can be used to create a sense of community, foster collaboration, and build relationships.

When engaging in mutual support, it is important to remember that everyone has something to offer and that everyone can benefit from the support of others. It is important to be respectful of each other's contributions and to recognize that everyone has something to gain from the collaboration. Mutual support can be used to create a sense of community, foster collaboration, and build relationships. It can also be used to develop problem-solving skills, increase self-confidence, and create a sense of belonging.

Mutual support is a powerful tool that can help individuals and groups alike to achieve their goals. It is a form of collaboration that involves individuals or groups working together to achieve a common goal. Mutual support can be used to build relationships, foster collaboration, and create a sense of community. By engaging in mutual support, individuals and groups can benefit from the knowledge, skills, and resources of one another, leading to greater success and satisfaction.

In order for mutual support to be effective, it is important for individuals to have a shared goal and to be open and honest with one another. This requires building trust and establishing clear communication, so that everyone can work together effectively. It also requires a willingness to help and support one another, as well as to give and receive constructive feedback.

There are many different ways in which mutual support can be fostered, including:

Building relationships: Engage in activities that help individuals get to know one another and build relationships, such as team-building exercises, shared experiences, and social events.

Sharing knowledge and resources: Encourage individuals to share their knowledge, skills, and resources with one another. This can be done through mentorship programs, peer-to-peer learning, and collaborative projects.

Encouraging collaboration: Encourage individuals to work together on projects and initiatives, and to seek out opportunities to collaborate with one another.

Recognizing and rewarding contributions: Acknowledge and celebrate the contributions of individuals and groups, and reward those who have made a significant impact through their support.

By engaging in mutual support, individuals and groups can build stronger relationships, improve their performance, and achieve their goals more effectively. Mutual support is a valuable tool that can be used to create a sense of community, foster collaboration, and drive success.

"Helping hands are the foundation of mutual support; they can create a powerful ripple effect of positive change."

ℬ

II

Understanding the Benefits of Mutual Support

Mutual support is a powerful tool that can help individuals and communities alike. It is a form of assistance that involves two or more people working together to achieve a common goal. Mutual support can take many forms, from providing emotional support to offering practical help. It is a valuable resource that can help people to overcome challenges, build relationships, and create a sense of belonging.

The benefits of mutual support are far-reaching. It can help to reduce stress and anxiety, improve mental health, and increase feelings of self-worth. It can also provide a sense of security and belonging, as well as a platform for sharing experiences and ideas. Mutual support can also help to build trust and foster collaboration between individuals and groups.

Mutual support can also be beneficial in terms of physical health. It can help to reduce the risk of developing chronic illnesses, such as heart disease and diabetes. It can also help to improve physical fitness and reduce the risk of injury. Additionally, mutual support can help to improve overall wellbeing, as it can provide a sense of purpose and connection.

Mutual support can also be beneficial in terms of financial stability. It can help to reduce the burden of financial stress, as well as provide access to resources and support. Additionally, mutual support can help to create a sense of financial security, as it can provide access to resources and support.

Finally, mutual support can help to create a sense of community. It can help to build relationships and foster collaboration between individuals and groups. It can also help to create a sense of belonging and connection, as well as provide a platform for sharing experiences and ideas.

In conclusion, mutual support is a powerful tool that can help individuals and communities alike. It can provide a sense of security and belonging, as well as a platform for sharing experiences and ideas. It can also help to reduce stress and anxiety, improve mental health, and increase feelings of self-worth.

In order to benefit from mutual support, it is important to cultivate a culture of openness and honesty, to build trust, and to establish clear communication. By engaging in mutual support and working together towards common goals, individuals and communities can achieve greater success and satisfaction.

Incorporating mutual support into your life can be as simple as reaching out to friends and family for help, joining a support group, or volunteering your time and resources to support a cause you believe in. By engaging in mutual support, we can all help to create a stronger, more connected, and more supportive world.

"Mutual support is a powerful force that can bring people together to make a positive difference in the world."

ᘓ

III

Exploring Mutual Support Groups

Mutual support groups are a powerful tool for individuals to come together and share their experiences, struggles, and successes. These groups provide a safe space for members to express themselves and receive support from their peers. Mutual support groups can be found in a variety of settings, from online forums to in-person meetings.

The benefits of mutual support groups are numerous. Members can gain insight into their own experiences and learn from the experiences of others. They can also find comfort in knowing that they are not alone in their struggles. Additionally, members can develop a sense of community and belonging, as well as build meaningful relationships with other members.

When exploring mutual support groups, it is important to consider the type of group that best suits your needs.

Different groups may have different focuses, such as mental health, addiction, or grief. It is also important to consider the size of the group, as well as the frequency of meetings.

When joining a mutual support group, it is important to be mindful of the group's expectations and guidelines. Respect for other members is paramount, and members should be mindful of the group's confidentiality policy. Additionally, members should be aware of their own boundaries and be prepared to take responsibility for their own actions.

The exploration of mutual support groups can be a powerful and rewarding experience. By joining a group, members can gain insight into their own experiences, build meaningful relationships, and find comfort in knowing that they are not alone. Mutual support groups can be a powerful tool for individuals to come together and share their experiences, struggles, and successes.

"The power of helping hands is that it can bring people together to achieve a common goal."

ꕥ

IV

Exploring the Role of Team Leadership

Teamwork is an essential part of any successful endeavor. It is the collective effort of individuals working together to achieve a common goal. Teams can be formed in any number of ways, from informal groups of friends to formal organizations. No matter the structure, teams are essential for the success of any project.

The role of teams in any endeavor is to provide support, guidance, and resources to help the team reach its goals. Teams can provide a sense of camaraderie and belonging, which can help to motivate members to work together. Teams can also provide a platform for members to share ideas and collaborate on solutions.

Teamwork is especially important in the context of mutual support. Mutual support is the idea that individuals can help each other to achieve their goals. This type of support can come in many forms, from providing emotional support to offering practical advice. Teams can provide a safe space for members to share their experiences and offer support to one another.

Teamwork can also help to foster a sense of accountability. When members of a team are held accountable for their actions, they are more likely to work together to achieve their goals. This can help to ensure that everyone is working towards the same goal and that the team is making progress.

Finally, teams can provide a sense of community. When members of a team come together to work towards a common goal, they can form strong bonds and create a sense of belonging. This can help to create a sense of purpose and motivation for members to continue working together.

Teamwork is an essential part of any successful endeavor, and it is especially important in the context of mutual support. Teams can provide a sense of camaraderie, accountability, and community, which can help to ensure that everyone is working towards the same goal. By working together, team members can leverage their strengths, pool their resources, and share the burden of workload, leading to better results and greater satisfaction.

Effective teamwork requires strong leadership, clear communication, and a shared understanding of goals and expectations. Team members must also be open and willing to collaborate, provide constructive feedback, and support one another.

In order to cultivate a successful and supportive team, it is important to:

Establish clear goals and expectations: Ensure that everyone on the team understands what is expected of them, and what the team is working towards.

Foster open and honest communication: Encourage team members to share their thoughts and ideas, and to provide constructive feedback to one another.

Encourage collaboration and teamwork: Create opportunities for team members to work together on projects and initiatives, and to support one another.

Recognize and reward individual and team contributions: Acknowledge and celebrate the achievements of individuals and the team as a whole, and reward those who have made a significant impact.

Foster a positive team culture: Encourage team members to support one another, build relationships, and create a sense of camaraderie and community.

By cultivating a supportive and collaborative team environment, individuals can achieve their goals more effectively and with greater satisfaction. Teamwork and mutual support go hand in hand, and are essential components of success in any endeavor.

"Mutual support is a powerful tool that can help us reach our goals and make a difference in the world."

ꕥ

V

Analyzing Mutual Aid Organizations

Mutual aid organizations are a powerful force in society, providing a wide range of services and support to those in need. From providing food and shelter to offering emotional and financial assistance, these organizations are essential to the well-being of many individuals and communities. This chapter will explore the various ways in which mutual aid organizations can be analyzed, including their structure, goals, and impact.

The structure of mutual aid organizations is an important factor to consider when analyzing them. These organizations are typically composed of volunteers who are dedicated to providing assistance to those in need. They may be organized into committees or teams, with each team focusing on a specific area of service. Additionally, mutual aid organizations may have a board of directors or other governing body that oversees the organization's operations. Understanding the structure of a mutual aid organization can help to identify its strengths and weaknesses.

The goals of mutual aid organizations are also important to consider when analyzing them. These organizations typically have a mission statement that outlines their purpose and objectives. This mission statement can provide insight into the organization's priorities and how it plans to achieve its goals. Additionally, understanding the organization's goals can help to identify potential areas of improvement.

Finally, the impact of mutual aid organizations should be considered when analyzing them. These organizations often provide essential services to those in need, such as food, shelter, and emotional support. Additionally, they may provide financial assistance or other resources to help individuals and communities in need. Examining the impact of mutual aid organizations can help to identify areas where they are making a positive difference and areas where they could be doing more.

In conclusion, analyzing mutual aid organizations is an important step in understanding their role in society. By examining their structure, goals, and impact, we can gain insight into how these organizations are helping to improve the lives of individuals and communities. Through mutual aid, individuals and communities can support one another, pool their resources, and work towards common goals.

It is clear that mutual aid organizations play a crucial role in addressing various social and economic challenges, particularly in times of crisis. However, they also face many challenges and limitations, including limited resources, lack of recognition, and difficulties in achieving sustainability.

Despite these challenges, the importance of mutual aid in society cannot be overstated. As individuals and communities face increasing economic and social challenges, it is clear that mutual aid will continue to play a vital role in addressing these issues and promoting greater equity and justice.

Therefore, it is important to continue to support and invest in mutual aid organizations, to ensure that they have the resources and support they need to continue their vital work. By doing so, we can help to build a more just and equitable society, where everyone has access to the resources and support they need to thrive.

"The impact of helping hands is that it can create a sense of community and belonging."

VI

Examining the Benefits of Parent Support Groups

Parent support groups can be a powerful tool for parents to gain insight, understanding, and support from other parents who are going through similar experiences. Examining the benefits of parent support groups can help us to better understand the impact of mutual support and the power of helping hands.

One of the primary benefits of parent support groups is the ability to connect with other parents who are going through similar experiences. By joining a support group, parents can share their stories, struggles, and successes with others who can relate. This can be a great source of comfort and understanding, as well as a way to gain valuable advice and tips from those who have been in similar situations.

Another benefit of parent support groups is the opportunity to learn from the experiences of others. By listening to the stories of other parents, we can gain insight into how they have handled similar situations and how they have coped with the challenges of parenting. This can be a great source of inspiration and motivation for parents who are struggling with their own parenting challenges.

In addition to providing emotional support, parent support groups can also provide practical advice and resources. Many groups offer workshops and seminars on topics such as parenting skills, child development, and family dynamics. These can be invaluable resources for parents who are looking for ways to better understand and support their children.

Finally, parent support groups can be a great way to build a sense of community. By joining a group, parents can form meaningful relationships with other parents and build a network of support. This can be a great way to stay connected and to find support when needed.

Overall, parent support groups can be a powerful tool for parents to gain insight, understanding, and support from other parents who are going through similar experiences. By joining a support group, parents can share their stories, struggles, and successes with others who can relate, learn from the experiences of others, gain access to valuable resources, and build a sense of community. Examining the benefits, structure, and impact of parent support groups can provide a deeper understanding of how these groups can benefit parents and their families.

Benefits of Parent Support Groups:

Emotional support: Being a parent can be a challenging and isolating experience, and a support group can provide a safe and supportive space for parents to share their emotions and feelings.

Knowledge sharing: By sharing their experiences with others, parents can learn about new strategies, techniques, and resources for raising children.

Increased confidence: By sharing their experiences and hearing the experiences of others, parents can gain confidence in their parenting skills and feel more equipped to handle challenges.

Access to resources: Support groups often have access to a variety of resources and information that can be useful to parents.

Sense of community: By joining a support group, parents can build relationships with other parents and feel a sense of belonging to a supportive community.

In order to maximize the benefits of parent support groups, it is important to choose a group that aligns with your needs and values. It is also important to be an active participant in the group, by sharing your experiences and supporting others.

In conclusion, parent support groups can be a valuable resource for parents who are looking for emotional support, knowledge sharing, and a sense of community. By joining a support group, parents can build stronger relationships with other parents, gain a deeper understanding of their experiences, and develop the skills and resources they need to succeed as a parent.

"Mutual support is a powerful force that can bring people together to make a positive impact."

ꟹ

VII

Understanding the Impact of Social Support

Social support is an essential part of life, and understanding its impact is key to living a healthy and fulfilling life. In this chapter, we will explore the power of social support and how it can help us to cope with life's challenges.

Social support is defined as the emotional, informational, and tangible assistance that we receive from our social networks. It can come in the form of family, friends, colleagues, and even strangers. Social support can be both direct and indirect, and it can be provided in a variety of ways. For example, a friend may offer emotional support by listening to your problems and offering advice. A colleague may provide informational support by sharing their knowledge and experience. And a stranger may provide tangible support by offering a helping hand.

The impact of social support is far-reaching. It can help us to cope with stress, build resilience, and even improve our physical health. Studies have shown that people who have strong social support networks are more likely to have better mental health, better physical health, and better overall wellbeing.

Social support can also help us to build relationships and foster a sense of belonging. It can provide us with a sense of security and comfort, and it can help us to feel connected to others. Studies have shown that people who have strong social support networks are more likely to have better relationships with their family and friends, and they are more likely to feel a sense of belonging in their communities.

Finally, social support can help us to achieve our goals. It can provide us with the motivation and encouragement we need to reach our goals, and it can help us to stay on track when we feel overwhelmed. Studies have shown that people who have strong social support networks are more likely to achieve their goals and to experience greater success in their lives.

In conclusion, social support is an essential part of life, and understanding its impact is key to living a healthy and fulfilling life. It can help us to cope with challenges, build resilience, and improve our overall well-being. Whether it comes from friends, family, or support groups, social support can provide us with the encouragement, accountability, and resources we need to achieve our goals and live a fulfilling life.

In order to benefit from social support, it is important to cultivate strong relationships and to seek out supportive networks. This can be done by actively seeking out supportive people in your life, participating in activities and events that bring you in contact with others, and being an active and supportive member of your community.

In summary, social support plays a crucial role in our lives and should not be underestimated. By seeking out and nurturing supportive relationships, we can improve our well-being, increase our chances of success, and lead more fulfilling and meaningful lives.

"The power of helping hands is that it can provide strength and hope in times of need."

ꟹ

VIII

Understanding the Role of Self-Help Groups

Self-help groups are a powerful tool for individuals to gain support and understanding from others who are facing similar challenges. These groups provide a safe space for members to share their experiences, learn from one another, and develop strategies for coping with their struggles. Self-help groups can be found in a variety of settings, including online forums, in-person meetings, and even virtual meetings.

Self-help groups can be beneficial for a variety of reasons. For one, they provide a sense of community and belonging. Members of self-help groups often develop strong bonds with one another, which can be a source of comfort and strength. Additionally, self-help groups can provide members with a sense of empowerment. By sharing their stories and experiences, members can gain insight into their own struggles and develop strategies for overcoming them.

Self-help groups can also be a great source of information. Members can learn about different coping strategies, resources, and treatments that may be beneficial for their particular situation. Additionally, members can gain insight into the experiences of others, which can help them to better understand their own struggles.

Finally, self-help groups can be a great source of motivation. By hearing the stories of others who have faced similar struggles, members can be inspired to take action and make positive changes in their lives. Additionally, members can gain support and encouragement from one another, which can be invaluable in times of difficulty.

Self-help groups can be a powerful tool for individuals to gain support, understanding, and motivation. By providing a safe space for members to share their stories and experiences, self-help groups can be a great source of comfort, empowerment, and inspiration. With the right support and guidance, self-help groups can be a powerful tool for individuals to make positive changes in their lives and to overcome challenges.

Self-help groups can be especially beneficial for those struggling with mental health issues, addiction, or other challenges. They can provide a supportive community where individuals can share their experiences and receive feedback, advice, and guidance from others who have been through similar experiences.

It is important to remember that self-help groups are not a substitute for professional help, and that individuals seeking help for serious mental health issues should consult with a licensed mental health professional. However, self-help groups can be a valuable supplement to professional treatment, and can provide individuals with a supportive community to help them stay on track and make progress towards their goals.

In summary, self-help groups can be a powerful tool for individuals seeking support, motivation, and understanding. By providing a supportive community and a safe space for individuals to share their experiences and learn from others, self-help groups can play an important role in helping individuals overcome challenges and make positive changes in their lives.

"Mutual support is a powerful reminder that we are all connected and can make a difference when we work together."

ᘓ

IX

Examining the Benefits of Professional Support

Professional support can be a powerful tool in helping individuals reach their goals and achieve success. Examining the benefits of professional support can provide insight into how it can be used to improve lives and create positive outcomes.

The power of professional support lies in its ability to provide individuals with the resources and guidance they need to reach their goals. Professional support can come in the form of counseling, mentoring, or coaching. Counseling can provide individuals with the tools and strategies they need to manage their emotions and behaviors. Mentoring can provide individuals with the guidance and support they need to develop their skills and reach their goals. Coaching can provide individuals with the motivation and accountability they need to stay on track and reach their goals.

Professional support can also provide individuals with the opportunity to gain insight into their own strengths and weaknesses. Through counseling, mentoring, or coaching, individuals can gain a better understanding of their own capabilities and how to use them to their advantage. Professional support can also provide individuals with the opportunity to develop their problem-solving skills and learn how to effectively manage their stress.

In addition to providing individuals with the resources and guidance they need to reach their goals, professional support can also provide individuals with the opportunity to build meaningful relationships. Through counseling, mentoring, or coaching, individuals can develop relationships with professionals who can provide them with the support and encouragement they need to reach their goals. Professional support can also provide individuals with the opportunity to build relationships with peers who can provide them with the support and encouragement they need to reach their goals.

The power of professional support lies in its ability to provide individuals with the resources and guidance they need to reach their goals. By examining the benefits of professional support, individuals can gain insight into how it can be used to improve their lives and create positive outcomes. Professional support can provide individuals with the tools and strategies they need to manage their emotions and behaviors, develop their skills, and build meaningful relationships. Ultimately, professional support can help individuals to achieve greater happiness, satisfaction, and success in their personal and professional lives.

In conclusion, professional support can be a valuable resource for individuals looking to achieve their goals and improve their lives. Whether it is through counseling, mentoring, or coaching, professional support provides individuals with the opportunity to receive the guidance, resources, and support they need to reach their full potential. By tapping into the power of professional support, individuals can experience greater success, happiness, and fulfillment in their lives.

"The impact of helping hands is that it can foster a sense of unity and collaboration."

ꙮ

X

Understanding the Role of Mutual Support in Mental Health

Mutual support is an essential component of mental health. It is the act of providing emotional, physical, and psychological support to one another in order to promote well-being. This type of support can come from family, friends, and even strangers. It is a powerful tool that can help individuals cope with difficult situations, build resilience, and foster a sense of belonging.

Understanding the role of mutual support in mental health is key to creating a supportive environment. Mutual support can be seen in many forms, such as providing emotional support, offering practical assistance, and providing a listening ear. It can also involve providing advice, offering encouragement, and providing a safe space to talk.

The power of mutual support lies in its ability to create a sense of connection and belonging. It can help individuals feel less isolated and more connected to their community. It can also provide a sense of security and comfort, which can be especially beneficial for those struggling with mental health issues.

Mutual support can also help individuals build resilience. It can provide a sense of hope and optimism, which can help individuals cope with difficult situations. It can also provide a sense of purpose and meaning, which can help individuals stay motivated and focused on their goals.

Finally, mutual support can help individuals develop a sense of self-worth and self-confidence. It can provide a sense of validation and acceptance, which can help individuals feel more secure in their own skin. It can also provide a sense of belonging, which can help individuals feel more connected to their community.

In conclusion, understanding the role of mutual support in mental health is essential for creating a supportive environment. It can provide a sense of connection, belonging, resilience, and self-worth. It can also help individuals cope with difficult situations and stay motivated and focused on their goals. Mutual support is a powerful tool that can help individuals foster a sense of well-being and promote mental health.

"Mutual support is a powerful source of inspiration that can help us reach our goals and make a positive impact."

XI

Exploring the Impact of Mutual Support on Society.

Mutual support has a powerful impact on society, and it is essential to explore this impact in order to understand its significance. Mutual support is defined as the exchange of resources, services, and assistance between individuals or groups in order to meet their needs. This type of support can take many forms, from providing emotional support to offering financial assistance.

The impact of mutual support on society is far-reaching. It can help to reduce poverty and inequality, as well as improve access to education and healthcare. It can also help to strengthen communities by providing a sense of belonging and connection. Mutual support can also help to foster a sense of trust and cooperation between individuals and groups, which can lead to greater understanding and collaboration.

Mutual support can also have a positive impact on mental health. Studies have shown that providing support to others can help to reduce stress and anxiety, as well as improve self-esteem and overall wellbeing. Additionally, mutual support can help to reduce the stigma associated with mental health issues, as it can provide a safe and supportive environment for individuals to discuss their struggles.

The impact of mutual support on society is also evident in the workplace. Studies have shown that providing support to colleagues can help to improve job satisfaction and productivity. Additionally, mutual support can help to create a more positive work environment, as it can foster a sense of trust and collaboration between employees.

Finally, mutual support can help to create a more inclusive society. By providing support to those who are marginalized or disadvantaged, mutual support can help to reduce discrimination and create a more equitable society.

In conclusion, mutual support has a powerful impact on society. It can help to reduce poverty and inequality, improve access to education and healthcare, strengthen communities, foster trust and collaboration, reduce stigma associated with mental health issues, improve job satisfaction and productivity, and create a more inclusive society. It is essential to explore the impact of mutual support in order to understand its significance and to ensure that everyone has access to the resources and support they need to achieve their goals and lead fulfilling lives. By promoting mutual support and encouraging individuals and communities to work together, we can create a more inclusive, equitable, and supportive society where everyone has the opportunity to thrive.

"The power of helping hands is that it can create a sense of belonging and connection."

"Mutual support is a powerful reminder that we are all in this together and can make a difference when we work together."

"The impact of helping hands is that it can bring people together to create a brighter future."

"Mutual support is a powerful tool that can help us reach our goals and make a lasting impact."

"The power of helping hands is that it can provide comfort and hope in times of need."

ဆ

OTHER BOOKS OF THE AUTHOR

1. The Moments When I Met God
2. Kashiyile Theertha Pathangal
3. GURU GYAN VANI
4. Abhiprerak Gita
5. ASSI SE JAIN GHAT TAK
6. Hopelessness of Arjuna
7. The Soul and It's True Nature
8. Sense of Action (Karma)
9. Action through Wisdom
10. Action through Wisdom
11. THEORY AND PRACTICAL OF EVERY ACTION
12. LOGICAL UNDERSTANDING OF THE SUPREME
13. THE IMPERISHABLE SUPREME
14. Yatra Nishadraj se Hanuman Ghat Tak
15. Yatra Karnatak Ghat se Raja Ghat Tak
16. Yatra Pandey Ghat se Prayagraj Ghat Tak
17. Yatra Ranjendra Prasad Ghat se Dattatreya Ghat Tak
18. YaatraSindhiya Ghat se Gwaliar Ghat Tak
19. Yatra Mangala Gauri Ghat se Hanuman Gadhi Ghat Tak
20. Yatra Gaay Ghat Se Nishad Ghat Tak
21. MAA GANGA, GHATEN EVM UTSAV
22. Ganga Arti Dev Deepavali evam Any Utsav
23. Potentials of Digitalized India
24. VEDIC CONSCIOUSNESS
25. A Brief Introduction to Vedic Science
26. Kashi ke Barah Jyotirling
27. IMPACT OF MOTIVATION
28. Let's have a Milky Way Journey
29. Color Therapy in a Nutshell

30. Rigveda in a Nutshell
31. Yajurveda in a Nutshell
32. Samveda in a Nutshell
33. Atharva Veda in a Nutshell
34. Ayushman Bhava - Ayurveda
35. Srimad Bhagavad Gita and Upanishad Connection
36. Srimad Bhagavad Gita - an attempt to summarize each chapter.
37. Facts and Impact of Nakshatra
38. Astro Gems - NAVARATNA
39. Ekadashi - A Concise Overview
40. A Concise View of Hanuman Chalisa
41. Inspirational Gita
42. Nakshatraranyam
43. Summary of 18 Mahapuranas
44. Synopsis of 18 Upa Puranas
45. Rigvediya Upanishads
46. Shukla Yajurvediya Upanishads
47. Krishna Yajurvediya Upanishads
48. Samavediya Upanishads
49. Atharvavediya Upanishads
50. The Seven Great Sages
51. From Rocket Scientist to President Dr. APJ Abdul Kalam
52. The Visionary's Voice - Quotes of Dr. APJ Abdul Kalam
53. The Wisdom of Swami Vivekananda: Insights and Inspiration from a Legendary Spiritual Teacher
54. Ayurvedic Remedies from the Garden
55. Sages and Seers
56. Rising Strong – Motivational Stories of Women
57. Beyond Flames -Mystery stories of Funeral Ghat Manikarnika
58. The Origins of Tulsi: A Look at the Mythological Roots of the Plant"

59. The Holistic Cow: A Look at the Physical, Spiritual, and Cultural Importance of Cows in India
60. Arts of Healing
61. Exploring the Divine
62. Understanding Five Elements
63. The Etymology of Ram
64. Symbols of India
65. Voice of Change (About Speeches of Great Men)
66. She Speaks (About Speeches of Great Women)
67. Patriotism on Celluloid – Brief About Patriotic Films
68. The Music of Motivation: A Brief Guide to Inspirational Film Songs
69. **Unlocking the Secrets of the Dashopanishads**
70. A Cultural Mosaic
71. Ancient Traditions, Modern Minds
72. Ecos of Ancient Wisdom
73. Beneath the Surface
74. From Temples to Ashrams
75. Sages of the Subcontinent
76. The Art of Healling (Ayurveda, Yoga & Naturopathy)
77. Indian Kitchen
78. The Festivals of India
79. The Indian Epics Retold
80. The Power of Mantras
81. The Indian River Ganges
82. The Indian Architecture
83. Rites of Passage
84. The Indian Silk Road
85. The Indian Literature
86. The Indian Villages
87. The Indian Folks & Crafts
88. The Way of Buddha
89. The Ramayan of Tulsidas

90. Astrological Remedies
91. The Secret Power of Motivation
92. Secret of Developing your Inner Strength
93. The Secret Path to Motivation
94. The Art and Secret of Positive Thinking
95. The Secrets of Practicing Ethical Living
96. Indian Art and Painting
97. The Indian Herbalism
98. Bharatanatyam to Kathak
99. Exploring India's Astrological Remedies
100. The Indian Festival of Flowers
101. Indian Handicrafts
102. The Splashes of Joy – India's Colour Festival
103. The Indian Science of Astrology
104. The Indian Mythology
105. Path to Enlightenment
106. The Indian Spirituality for Children
107. Aromas of India
108. The Secrets of Healthy Relationships
109. Ancestral Ties
110. The Indian Street Food
111. Discovering America
112. The Indian Textile
113. Listening to Motivational Speeches
114. Taste of India
115. A Cultural Journey through Indian Nuptials
116. Motivational Quote for Change
117. Secret Strategies for Making Money
118. Secrets to Cultivate a Positive Mindset
119. A Tapestry of Cultures: Exploring India from Kashmir to Kanyakumari
120. Achieving Your Dreams with Resilience: Secret Strategies for Overcoming Obstacles

121. Innovative Startups - 25 Startup Ideas to Spark Your Business Creativity
122. Export Management: Strategies for Global Success
123. Exporting from India - A Step by Step Guide
124. Finance Fundamentals: Mastering Financial Management for Business Success
125. Global Growth Strategies for International Business Development
126. Marketing Mastery: Unlocking the Secrets of Modern Marketing
127. Operations Mastery: Managing the Flow of Value in Business
128. Strategic Business Management: Navigating the Modern Business Landscape
129. Human Resource Management Strategies for Building and Managing a High Performance Team
130. The Indian Landscapes and Nature: An Exploration Of India's Natural Beauty And Diversity
131. The Indian Street Performances: A Cultural Exploration of India's Street Performances
132. Affirming Your Self-Worth: Strategies for Achieving Emotional Wellbeing
133. Cultivating Self-Discipline: Secrets Methods for Achieving Your Goals
134. Embracing Change: Strategies for Adapting to Life's Challenges
135. Embracing Your Uniqueness: Secret Strategies for Living an Authentic Life
136. Finding Motivation in Despondency: Coping with Difficult Times
137. Embracing Change
138. Learning to Love Yourself
139. Managing Time for Yourself

140. Unlock the keys to Self-Motivation
141. Secret to Boost Confidence
142. Unlocking your Potential: A Path to Inner-strength & Success
143. Secrets to Develop Authentic Relationship
144. Secrets to Build a Successful Career
145. Secrets to Live with Gratitude
146. Secrets to Create a Life of Abundance
147. Secrets to Cultivate Self-Awareness
148. The Power of Helping Hands
149. Finding Your Passion
150. The Indian Mythical Creatures
151. The Indian Women Saints
152. The Wisdom of the Saints
153. "The Indian Royalty: A Cultural and Historical Exploration of India's Maharajas and their kingdom"
154. The Mystic Land: A Cultural and Spiritual Exploration of India"

CONTACT

DR. JAGADEESH PILLAI

MBA & PhD in Vedic Science

Four Times Guinness World Record Holder

Winner of Mahatma Gandhi Vishwa Shanti Puraskar and
Global Peace Ambassador

Gemology, Astro & Vastu Consultant - Spiritual Counselor

Consultant for designing World Record Ideas

Efficient Tarot Card Reader

9839093003

myrichindia@gmail.com

drjagadeeshpillai@facebook

drjagadeeshpillai@instagram
jagadeeshpillai@youtube

www. JAGADEESHPILLAI.com

ꙮ

|| LOKAHA SAMASTHAHA SUKHINO BHAVANTU ||

9 798889 595359

Printed by Libri Plureos GmbH in Hamburg,
Germany